PROFILES OF DISASTER-PRONE RELATIONSHIPS:

How to Detect, Avoid, Survive or Escape Them

Dr. Minnie Claiborne

Profiles of Disaster-prone Relationships by Dr. Minnie Claiborne

ISBN 978-1-952027-22-2 (Paperback)
ISBN 978-1-952027-23-9 (Hardback)

This book is written to provide information and motivation to readers. Its purpose is not to render any type of psychological, legal, or professional advice of any kind. The content is the sole opinion and expression of the author, and not necessarily that of the publisher.

Copyright © 2020 by Dr. Minnie Claiborne

All rights reserved. No part of this book may be reproduced, transmitted, or distributed in any form by any means, including, but not limited to, recording, photocopying, or taking screenshots of parts of the book, without prior written permission from the author or the publisher. Brief quotations for noncommercial purposes, such as book reviews, permitted by Fair Use of the U.S. Copyright Law, are allowed without written permissions, as long as such quotations do not cause damage to the book's commercial value. For permissions, write to the publisher, whose address is stated below.

Printed in the United States of America.

New Leaf Media, LLC
175 S. 3rd Street, Suite 200
Columbus, OH 43215
www.thenewleafmedia.com

Also By Dr. Minnie Claiborne

Prayer Therapy-Stop Hurting

Read and Pray Through the Bible

Stop Searching...Start Attracting

This book is dedicated to women and men who dare to still believe in love

CONTENTS

Finally, the book you've been waiting for

1. Disastrous Relationship
2. Profiles of Some Disastrous Relationships
3. Flaw or Fault?
4. Profile of An Abuser
5. Are You Relationship Ready?
6. Take Care of Your Own Garden
7. Meaning of The 7 Secrets
8. Take My Relationship -Readiness Challenge
9. 7 Secrets Relationship Profiler
10. Components of a Good Relationship
11. 12 Relationship Killers: 18 Traits of Great Relationships
12. Beware of Depression
13. Ask Dr. Minnie
    a. Am I A Sex Addict
    b. Is Jesus My Husband?
    c. Do Men Have A Stronger Sex Drive Than Women?
    d. Does the Good Outweigh the Bad?
    e. How Soon Should I Have Sex?
    f. Cheaters
    g. Naïve
    h. Commit or Not Commit
    i. Liar
    j. What Oprah Said
    k. Happily Married?

CHAPTER 1

Disastrous Relationship

I usually remember the things that I get wrong. I will forever remember how to spell receive because I lost a spelling bee when I was 13 years old when I misspelled it. I spelled received, *recieved*. I wish that making one mistake in the area of relationships and forever getting it right thereafter was as easy as correcting a spelling error. It is not. When it comes to successful interpersonal, particularly romantic relationships, most of us have missed it a time or two or three or four or more....

The first time I missed the mark in a relationship, I knew to avoid making the same mistake in the next one. Intelligent, naïve, trusting, country-bumpkin me; I carefully avoided a partner who displayed dysfunctions A-B-C. But alas, the next couple of individuals had dysfunctions C-D-F and R-O-Q. Never heard of those? Neither had I. Just because you avoid one set of dysfunctions in an individual is no guarantee that the next person will not have something else that you were totally unexpecting and unprepared to handle.

Not all of my relationships have been disastrous. Thank God, I have had wonderful relationships with men who loved me and treated me very, very well. Those relationships helped to serve as reminders of how I deserve to be treated.

At the time that I chose disaster-prone relationships, my life circumstances and experiences made me vulnerable. In retrospect I was too trusting. I relinquished too much of my power.

Sarah Jakes Roberts -- daughter of renowned pastor, movie producer and T.V. host, T.D. Jakes -- became pregnant at age 13. Drowning in low self-esteem, she married a man who was toxic and abusive. It took several years for her to forgive herself, regain her dignity and position herself to make a healthier relationship choice. One of my greatest aims in this book is to help empower or re-empower you to be the best you, so that you can make the best choices for you.

My good friend, Laurie Hunter, said this to me during a low period in my life.

Sister, hold your head up so your crown won't fall off

I have met and counseled far too many individuals, especially women, whose crowns of self-esteem, crowns of self-worth and crowns of dignity have fallen off. Some do not know what it looks like or feels like to be treated well by a man. Many have de-dignified (my word) themselves and lost all semblance of self-worth and self-esteem. You have to get that restored! A relationship cannot fix you. Some deficiencies make us vulnerable, other deficiencies and experiences make us unable to sustain a good, healthy relationship. Some behaviors are "relationship killers"; others are literally fatal. Am I in the minority in thinking that relationships are supposed to be composed of two human beings who are basically emotionally and mentally healthy and compatible? Is it too much to expect that, when two people make a commitment or vow in marriage to each other, there should be mutual respect, honesty, integrity, love and support, at least minimally?

In both my personal and professional life, I have observed an unprecedented amount of deception, pain, fear, destruction and devastation in relationships that promised love, happiness and a future. This epidemic of devastation is destroying individuals, families, communities, cities, even nations. The repercussions, like the ripples from a rock thrown into a pond, are destroying generations. On a weekly basis, I deal with individuals who were wounded in childhood by adult dysfunctions.

I am not writing this book as an expert who has not been touched by this disease in relationships. Both I, and especially my children, have suffered, and still deal with the ripples of pain from the rocks and pebbles in the ponds of negative, painful experiences of my wrong choices in relationships. I pray for us every day.

Let me specify. My helping, forgiving, nurturing personality, along with my childhood love deficiencies, certainly predisposed and caused me to be vulnerable in certain areas. Vulnerability is a flaw that opens you up to attack and damage. It caused me to be victimized, but it is not necessarily in itself a "relationship killer". However, it was a factor because it predisposed me to accept relationships without properly vetting or profiling them. Another factor that influenced my choices is that I was not my "best self" when I made them. I am appalled at the number of individuals who can count 10, 20, 30 years of marriage, but only because at least one of the partners has accepted mistreatment or horrifying disrespect, disregard, and destruction throughout the duration of the marriage. Some die prematurely from the stress. Some finally escape, but they are emotionally and mentally bloodied, battered, traumatized, devoid of self-esteem and self-identity.

According to William Pinsof, Ph.D., *"Divorce has replaced death as the primary terminator of marriage. It has become a "normal" marital end point"*. When we hear of the dissolution of a marriage of 10, 20 or 30 years, we often wonder why did they break up after all of those years of a happy marriage? I submit that it was not a happy marriage. Those years were the saturation point of pain for one or both partners. Someone simply could not bear it any longer. Bishop

Steve Harvey wrote a wonderful book, *Act Like A Lady, Think Like A Man*. He does a good job of helping women to find love and work toward getting married. Getting married seems to be the prevailing obsession for many, many people, particularly women. This is natural and understandable. Unfortunately, marriage is too often, *the beginning of sorrows.* This should not be so.

Once you do get married, are you and your partner strong enough to withstand the inevitable, unanticipated storms of life that will test your souls and the soul of your relationship?

In this book, *Profiles of Disaster-Prone Relationships: How to Detect, Avoid , Survive or Escape Them,* you will embark on a journey into the lives and scenarios of different people in the hope that you learn how to discover pitfalls and avoid them.

Were there warning signs that these people missed? Are there certain key questions that they failed to ask a potential partner? What's the difference between a flaw and a fault? How much can you probe without being offensive? How did people survive or escape disastrous relationships, and can you do the same? In this book, you will learn some of the traits, warning signs, behaviors and habits that you need to discern so that you can quickly *profile* a potential partner, as well as test your own personal relationship readiness.

By using my simple "7 Secrets Profile Assessment," you can measure your personal relationship readiness. For instance, what is your *relationship temperature?* Is your relationship healthy and strong? Then, call the bridesmaids or the cruise director. Does it need surgery? Call the doctor. Is it too sick to survive? Call the coroner. My assessment tool will enable you to quickly answer these questions. This book cannot guarantee you relationship success; you and your partner will determine that. However, this book can empower, inform, enhance, and equip you to have a happy, healthy and well-balanced personal life. It will provide simple, yet powerful tools that help you make intelligent, informed relationship choices and decisions. It can greatly increase your likelihood of relationship success and happiness.

Without endorsing anyone's lifestyle, philosophy or religion, I have sprinkled a few quotable quotes throughout the book from people who have shared their wisdom publicly. These include quotes from Maya Angelou, Carol Burnett, Viktor E. Frankel, Tamron Hall, Steve Harvey, Bishop T.D. Jakes, Joel Osteen, Gerald Riggs, Toure' Roberts, Sarah Jakes Roberts, Sherri Sheppard, and Oprah Winfrey.

"Only I can change my life, no one can do it for me"

Carol Burnett

CHAPTER 2

Profiles of Some Disastrous Relationships

Gregg and Rachel

She was 15 years old, the new girl in town, the new girl at school. All of the boys in the neighborhood wanted to check her out. She was settling into her homeroom class on this particular morning. A group of boys came to her class room door and pointed her out to Gregg. He stared at her so long and hard, the other boys had to pull him away. She found out later that at first sight, he fell in love with her and decided that she was going to be his wife.

During the school year and over the summer vacation, Gregg pursued Rachel. She finally gave in to the attention that he lavished on her. Besides, he was cute and had a winning smile. He was one of the popular boys at school. Lots of girls liked him, but Rachel was the girl for him.

Throughout high school, their love and devotion to each other were evident to everyone who saw them. They had a few break-ups, but everyone knew that Rachel was Gregg's girl. Once during a brief break-up another boy was trying to talk to Rachel. Gregg gave the boy a bloody nose. They always got back together. He was always there for her. He told her that he loved her dozens of times a day. He treated her like his precious doll. They would kiss for hours, but he never asked her for sex. It was true love.

Gregg and Rachael got married right after high school. About 3 weeks after they were married, Rachael began getting dressed one Sunday morning. Gregg asked her where she was going. "It's Sunday, she exclaimed, I'm going to church." Gregg had a job and would be at work that day.

Out of nowhere, Rachael suddenly felt a blinding, stinging slap across her face. She tasted blood on her lips. Stunned and confused, she looked into Gregg's glaring eyes and felt his hot breath as he growled, "You're my wife now. You're not going anywhere!"

For the next four years Rachael endured the heartbreak of Gregg's emotional and physical abuse. Her life became a living hell at times. Most of the time he was the loving, attentive, guy that she fell in love with, but the abuse always came. It happened for any reason or for no reason. She finally escaped with her life and divorced Gregg. Rachael had to begin her life as a young divorced mother of their 3-year-old daughter.

Is there any way Rachael could have seen this coming?

Jim and Tessa

Jim, 32, married a beautiful woman who was a covert cocaine addict. She was covert only until the honeymoon. Life was hell for 3 long, tortuous years while Jim co-dependently tried to hang in there, be supportive and make the marriage work. It didn't. When she began disappearing for 3 weeks at a time, instead of the usual 3 or 4 days, he could no longer stand the stress. I heard a preacher say once, "If you've been bitten by a snake, run at the sight of a worm." In other words, Jim knew to avoid anyone who was addicted to anything.

Because of his last disastrous relationship, Jim knew to avoid anyone with any symptoms of addictions.

NOTE: I describe addiction as almost like having another person or entity in a family. Family members must interact with each other, and they have to interact with the addiction. Obviously, those who suffer from addictions are rarely able to function properly. The family dynamic is almost completely disorganized. I have worked with clients who were able to somehow function successfully on their jobs in spite of being alcoholics. However, their relationships with their spouses and families were in shambles.

Back to Jim - four years after his divorce, he met and fell in love with another beautiful woman, Tessa. He played it smart this time. He carefully watched how much wine she drank on dinner dates. He noticed if she disappeared into the bath room too often while they were visiting friends. She even stayed at his parent's home for 3 days during a Thanksgiving holiday. His "one addict knows another addict" cousin, Andy, checked her out and pronounced her clean. Jim wisely checked for all of the signs. He went as far as to inquire about her from her relatives. She had no substance addictions. She was a very nice person. Hallelujah!

After 9 months of dating, Jim knew that Tessa was the one. He even respected the fact that her Christian faith influenced her to not have sex before marriage. As an extra measure, they attended a 10- week pre-martial class. Jim and Tessa had a beautiful wedding, and from their home in Ft. Lauderdale, Florida, took a honeymoon cruise to the islands.

Believe it or not, again on the honeymoon, poor Jim had an unpleasant surprise. Tessa had been horribly molested as a child and raped 8 years prior to the time that she met Jim. She began screaming and having heart palpitations when they tried to consummate their marriage. Tessa could not have intercourse with her beloved! Jim did not choose a woman with an addiction, but she had post-traumatic stress disorder (PTSD). Of course Tessa disclosed that she had been raped, but she did not know that she still suffered serious residual trauma from the experience. She had not been sexually active since the event had occurred and thought she had put the horrible incident behind her.

Poor Jim. How could he have known? How could she have known? How can you and I know?

Mary Craig Rice

I bet that 37 year old Mary Craig Rice regrets the day that she ever met Billy Boyette. After knowing him for only a few weeks, her life is forever changed. The evening news captured her desperate eyes as they darted around like those of a caged animal with no place to run. She appeared terrified, traumatized, shocked, devastated, abused and confused. Boyette killed 3 people, then shot and killed himself. Mary Rice was charged as an accomplice and possibly faces the death penalty.

How could something this horrible have happened?

Andrew and Katie

Andrew 35, was fascinated by Katie's subtle beauty, her warm smile and long, flowing hair. After dating for a year, they got married. Within 4 months of marriage, she could no longer hide her extreme mood swings and vicious, fiery tongue. For 7 years Andrew endured emasculating verbal and physical abuse from Katie. The marriage ended in divorce.

Why didn't he see it coming?

Alice

Alice told me that all of her relationships have been disastrous. She has been married 4 times. Alice has experienced some of the most devastating examples of betrayal, adultery and disrespect. One of her husband's mistresses burned their house down because she was enraged at him. She was at the hospital and watched another woman give birth to her husband's baby.

When I asked her why she stayed in that relationship for 13 years, she told me that she had 6 children. She knew that she could not provide and care for them by herself. She stayed for the sake of her children. Her husband was a pastor.

Were there pre-warning signs? What did she miss and why?

Other Disastrous Relationships

I helped Dr. Betty Price write her book entitled, *A Warning to Ministers, Their Mistresses and Their Wives*. The true accounts of spousal abuse and adultery by men who call themselves pastors are astonishing. Dr. Price's daughter, Angela, spoke on the subject at the Faith Dome. She read a letter from a woman who is married to a pastor. He had abused her with anal sex for so long that she had to wear diapers because her rectum was permanently damaged. She stayed with him because he used the Bible out of context to control her.

What can she do?

One lady told me that her husband's mistress killed him, leaving her to raise 7 children by herself. Another young woman and her children had to bear the shame of her husband's scandalous death. He had a heart attack while having sex with another woman. What a legacy to leave. What can you say at a funeral like that?

A woman on the East Coast described to me how for 2 years, her husband locked her in an attic. She was only allowed out to use the bathroom while he accompanied her at gunpoint.

There are too many disastrous relationships to describe. The devastation is all around us, in the news, in our neighborhoods, in our families. The problem not only devastates the victimized partner, it wreaks havoc on innocent children. They often grow up feeling angry, neglected, confused and unloved. Both males and females are often abused physically, emotionally, mentally and sexually. How can they function in a healthy manner in their relationships? The problem is escalating. It seems as if our society is imploding. A large part of it is because of disastrous relationships.

Some Disastrous Relationships Are Fatal

There are thousands, millions of stories of disastrous relationships, some are even fatal. In fact, death and abuse by a significant other is the most common cause of unnatural death to women. Check the FBI statistics or watch TV crime shows such as Forensic Files or Investigation ID.

Popular television journalist Tamron Hall has publicly shared how her sister Renate's brutal death has made her extremely cautious when it comes to dating and relationships. After years of relationships with abusive men, Renate's body was found brutally beaten and floating face down in the small backyard pool of her home in Houston, Texas, in 2004. The murder is still unsolved. Could a profiling tool have helped Renate?

I recently interviewed a lady on my television show. Her name is Davana Tinsley. She carries a huge picture of her murdered daughter when she speaks on domestic violence. Her 23-year-old daughter was stabbed 32 times, drowned in a bathtub and set on fire by her boyfriend. Wouldn't a monster like that be easy to spot? Maybe not.

Alvin and Anita

Alvin and Anita met at work. They were both attorneys. The attraction was strong and immediate. They found each other easy to talk to. Soon they were in a hot and heavy romantic relationship. There was one big problem however: Alvin was married. He had started a relationship with Anita during a trying time in his 5 year marriage to his wife, Joan. He had even hinted that he wanted to divorce his wife and marry her.

After 6 months with Anita, Alvin was ready to break it off and reconcile with his wife Joan. The couple had just found out that Joan was pregnant with their first child. This infuriated Anita. She became obsessive. She stalked Alvin, threatened him and tried to make his life a living hell. Unable to let go, Anita's disturbed mind, began to focus on Joan. In her mind, the only thing that stood between her and Alvin was Joan! One night, Anita did the unthinkable. She laid in wait and attacked Joan with a knife, stabbing her multiple times. Anita concentrated her stabs in Joan's heart, face and stomach. By then, Joan was 4 months pregnant.

Was this horrible tragedy avoidable?

A Well-Known Disastrous Relationships

Oscar and Reeva

For some reason, I became fascinated with the story of Oscar Pistorius, the South African sprinter. He was once an international icon and role-model, a champion despite having both of his legs amputated below the knees. He wears unusual prosthetic legs that look like sculpted blades. Pistorius is now a convicted killer, known as "the blade killer". If you've followed the story, you know that he shot and killed his super-model, girlfriend, Reeva Steenkamp, 6 times while she crouched behind a locked bathroom door. Here were two young, successful people who had a great future ahead of them. What happened? Was Reeva blinded by Oscar's star status and money, so captivated by his attention and charm that she rationalized his *dark-side*? Does this happen to other people?

Perhaps due to cultural influences, research indicates that males are typically the most frequent perpetrators of behaviors that are relationship destroyers. This does not dismiss the many instances of females who exhibit behaviors that cause relationships to be disastrous. Females commit adultery, kill their men, abuse their children, commit incest, just as males do, howbeit, not as commonly. Iconic beauties such as Elizabeth Taylor and many other women in public have been reported to commit adultery, become addicted to drugs and alcohol, and participate in other relationship-destroying behaviors. Whether male or female, it is usually the "unknown factors" that cause the victimized partners in disastrous relationships to be blindsided. I will refer back to our profiled couples as we continue our discussion.

NOTE: In intimate partner violence, about 15% of victims are men. This is not to be ignored. Abused men are more reluctant to report abuse because of traditional social norms where men are supposed to be dominant. However, by far 85% of the victims of domestic violence or intimate partner violence is perpetrated by men. The astonishing thing that makes this so reprehensible is researchers estimate that 96% of domestic violence would be prevented if MEN who are abusers would get the help that they need. This is a curable epidemic. If you are a perpetrator, you were probably once a victim of some sort. You can change. Abusive behavior constitutes a *fault*, not a flaw. It is something that you choose not to change even though you are destroying other people.

This book can serve as a beginning for you. I'm sure that when God created you, and your mother birthed you, it was not their dream, expectation or intention that you would grow up to be an abuser. You have no right to terrorize, control, dominate, intimidate and destroy other people's lives.

The women, children, and family members in your life, and God your Creator expect you to be the man you were created be. Get help!

"NO ONE HAS THE RIGHT TO DO WRONG, NOT EVEN IF WRONG HAS BEEN DONE TO THEM."

Viktor Frankl, Psychiatrist, Holocaust Survivor

One day, a few days after the liberation, I walked through the country past flowering meadows. Larks rose to the sky and I could hear their joyous song. There was no one to be seen for miles around; there was nothing but the wide earth and sky and the larks' jubilation and the freedom of space.

I stopped, looked around, and up to the sky-and then I went down on my knees. At that moment there was very little I knew of myself or the world-I had but one sentence in mind -always the same: "I called to the Lord from my narrow prison and He answered me in the freedom of space."

How long I knelt there and repeated this sentence- memory can no longer recall. But I know that on that day, in that hour, my new life started.

Step by step, I progressed, until I again became a human being.

Viktor Frankl

Everyone has flaws, you have to decide which flaws you can live with"

Steve Harvey

CHAPTER 3

Flaw or Fault?

The **definition** of a **flaw** is a mark or error that makes something faulty (imperfect)

An example of a **flaw** is a scratch on a gem.

Fault is a negligent or intentional failure to act reasonably or according to **law** or duty. It is an improper act or omission causing injury to another.

I chose to use the legal definitions of flaw and fault. In assessing ourselves and in profiling relationships or potential relationships, we need to be able to discern between a flaw and a fault. This may sometimes be subjective, but there are some key words and phrases that can help us to make a distinction between a flaw and a fault.

According to the above definitions, a flaw is an imperfection. As Steve Harvey so wisely stated, everyone has flaws. However, I think that in an effort to "not judge anyone", we have abdicated our intuition and discernment, our gut-feelings and hunches. These innate endowments may well be our best gauges for decision making. Incredibly, I have heard many people say, "deep down, I knew it was wrong, but I did it anyway". The most amazing are the ones who say, "God told me not to marry him or her, and I did it anyway." If that's you, ask for forgiveness sincerely, and let's move forward. We have to keep living.

A flaw can be corrected or in many cases, accepted or tolerated. A flaw can be very annoying, but is not necessarily a *relationship killer*. Flaws can range from minor to serious. I think that in some cases, the difference between a flaw and a fault is determined by the attitude of the individual. If a seriously flawed individual is humble enough to sincerely seek and pursue change, a partner may be able to exercise the necessary love and patience that are essential to work toward and support change.

I am not talking about the empty promises that are selfishly motivated. Some people will say anything in order to get what they want. Their sincerity can be determined by their actions.

Examples of flaws could be a partner who picks his or her nose or who snores, who is habitually late, leaves clothes where they take them off, a bad cook, has stinky feet, laughs too loud, talks with a mouth full of food and etc. A flaw can be an annoying habit. These can be more serious things such as a partner who has anxiety attacks, a partner who has health issues, or depression. If the core of that person is good and kind, the flaws can be corrected or tolerated.

Let's compare this with the definition of a fault. A fault is a **negligent** or **intentional** failure to act reasonably or according to **law** or duty. It is an improper act or omission **causing injury to another**. That definition is pretty serious and very scary when applied to the attitudes and behaviors of an individual. A person who has faults can be potentially dangerous, even deadly.

Negligent and intentional indicate a selfish, non-caring, non-empathetic person who does not care if he or she hurts someone else. This individual has no regard for the laws of God or man. They are filled with pride and seek self-gratification.

The problem here is that a person who is so obviously dark would cause most people to flee far from them. However, the individuals who have such deep faults conceal them until they have an emotional, sexual, financial, mental or legal stronghold on another person. They are wolves in sheep's clothing. They are masters of deception and disguise.

A person who encounters this type of individual may sense something but dismisses it, thinking they're being overly suspicious. After all, he takes me to nice places, buys me gifts, tells me he loves me and actually started me talking about moving in together or getting married after only a short time of knowing each other. She calls me every day at work to see what I want her to cook me for dinner, she even cleans my apartment, and she's beautiful!

Some of the behaviors that I would classify as a fault and probably relationship killers are: violent, abusive behavior, possessive jealousy, anger and rage, drug and alcohol addiction, adultery, sexual lust and incest, greed, deceitfulness, lying, irresponsible and blatantly not fulfilling the commitment, men not being providers, gambling and other addictions, untreated serious mental illness, engaging in illegal behaviors, unloving, not affectionate, and other destructive behaviors.

Many women and some men are natural nurturers. Some are co-dependent. These individuals are often drawn into a faulty relationship because of their caring, tolerant natures. Be aware, you may be a care-giver by profession and by nature, but to live with a person who persists in the behaviors that I have just described is virtual suicide. The stress of being exposed to such behaviors in a relationship 24/7 takes extreme grace, and could literally destroy you. Many times, some of these faults may happen because of certain unfortunate situations. In such cases, you will need survival tools in order to preserve your soul and your sanity. In the cases of abusive relationships, wisdom and support are essential. You will find information and resources in this book.

Let's take a look at the relationships described in chapter 2. Take the case of **Alvin and Anita.** Here were two successful, professionals who seriously broke some universal and relationship rules. They entered into an adulterous relationship. All lives involved were destroyed. Anita was not just flawed; she had serious faults. She committed adultery with a married man, she was possessively jealous, and she had rage and anger. The result, she murdered Alvin's wife and unborn baby. Instead of enjoying life as a successful lawyer, she was sentenced to life in prison. Alvin had the faults of adultery and lust. He now has to live with the fact that his careless, selfish actions caused the death of his wife and child. What answer can he give Anita's mother, her siblings, their friends, and his former colleagues? He was fired from his law firm.

How about **Jim and Tessa**? Jim, whose first wife was a cocaine addict, was extremely careful in selecting Tessa as his new wife. Their courtship was fun, respectful and solid. However, on their honeymoon, a new nightmare emerged. Tessa had been raped in the past and could not sexually consummate their marriage. Was this a flaw or a fault? I would consider this a flaw. Tessa did not set out to deceive Jim. She was not aware that she had PTSD. Although this is a serious disorder, this couple worked together, got good professional counseling and now enjoy a good marriage. In fact walking through this experience brought them closer together.

In the very sad case of **Oscar and Reeva**, it appears that they had the typical abusive, co-dependent relationship. Based on the information that was made public, Reeva was flawed. Oscar had serious faults. Reeva probably did not recognize the warning signs, and Oscar probably was not aware of how egregious his faults were. I feel very badly for both of them. Women like Reeva have flaws that make them vulnerable. The flaw can be a virtue in selecting a fulfilling profession; but if we are not careful and discerning it will make us susceptible to tolerating behaviors that we should not tolerate in personal relationships. Reeva felt sorry for Oscar, he was lonely. When he was good to her, he was very good. There was passion and promise in their relationship. She confronted his anger and possessiveness, but she did not draw proper boundaries. Based on the information from the news media, Oscar perfectly fit the profile of an abuser.

When someone shows you who they really are, believe them the first time.

Maya Angelou

CHAPTER 4

Profile of An Abuser: What I Wish Renate, Reeva, and Mary Had Known

Please read carefully. According to FBI and national statistics:

- 10 million people a day are killed by an intimate partner or ex-partner, approximately 20 people per minute
- 94% are females
- A large number of these are teenagers and young adult women
- 19.3 million women and 5.1 million men are stalked each year
- 90% of children in these relationships witness the violence and abuse

Don't be deceived! It can happen to *you* or anyone you know. What are the warning signs?

Warning Signs of a Domestic Abuser

If we can recognize the warning signs of a domestic abuser, or someone who is likely to have an abusive personality, we can save ourselves (and our loved ones) a lot of grief and heartache. Many survivors of abusive relationships have so often said that if they had just known the warning signs, they would never have gotten involved with their abusive partner.

The good news is, that it is possible to predict the likelihood of the person you are currently with or are about to become involved with being a domestic abuser. It is simply a matter of having the knowledge of the warning signs to look out for and being sufficiently aware to notice them (which includes not being too blinded by love, lust or desperation!).

Below are a list of behaviors, traits and beliefs which are common in abusive personalities. These are commonly known as "**Warning Signs of Abusive Personalities**" While not all abusive people show the same traits, or display the tendencies to the same extent, if several behavioral traits are present, there is a strong tendency toward abusiveness. Generally, the more warning signs are present, the greater the likelihood of violence. In some cases, an abuser may have only a couple of behavioral traits that can be recognized, but they are very exaggerated (e.g. extreme jealousy over ridiculous things).

Often the domestic abuser will initially try to explain his/her behavior as signs of his/her love and concern, and the victim may be flattered at first; as time goes on, the behaviors become more severe and serve to dominate, control and manipulate the victim.

Extreme Jealousy

A person who is abusive will try to excuse their behavior as a sign of how much they love you. He or she will try to control who you talk to, where you go, and will seek to isolate you from friends and family. As the jealousy and insecurity progresses, he/she may call or show up where you are unexpectedly. You may love the attention initially, but you may soon feel smothered.

Controlling

The abusive personality will explain away their undesirable behavior. They have been called 'crazy-makers' . They try to convince you that their controlling behavior is normal, and is because of their concern and care for you. Beware when you begin to feel as if you are losing yourself, and someone else is taking over your life. The abuser may become extremely jealous and angry if you are late, out with friends, or anything that appears to be an independent decision that you make. Remember the case of Gregg and Rachael. He slapped her hard across her face because she told him that she was going to church.

Quick Involvement

Gregg felt that it was love at first sight when he saw Rachael. He pursued her until he dominated her life and time. Many victims of abuse knew their abuser for less than six months before they were engaged or living together.

Abusers commonly play on the sympathy of the victim. They often claim that the victim is the only one that understands them. They 'play the victim' to gain sympathy from the person who is the object of their obsession. The abuser will often declare that you are 'made for each other', or that you are the only person whom he could ever talk to so open.

Isolation

The abuser wants to control how you think and behave. He or she will seek to isolate you from friends and families so that they will have no input or influence in your life. He/she will not want you to do anything or go anywhere separate from him or her. He/she may accuse you of being 'tied to your mother's apron strings' or say that friends or family members are trying to ruin your relationship.

Blaming Others

Have you every met some one who refuses to take responsibility for his or her own behavior? Individuals with abusive personality will rarely take responsibility for their negative behavior. They will shift the blame to you, someone else, or the situation. It is always someone else's fault. They will even blame you for their abusive behavior toward you. Remember the example that I referenced. The abuser shot his girlfriend 14 times, and yelled at her dead body as he was being handcuffed police, he yelled to her lifeless body, "now look what you made me do!"

Hypersensitive

Most abusers are easily insulted or upset. They have low self-esteem, so if you disagree with them in any way, they feel criticized or attacked. Many have a victim mentality and seem to always have an enemy.

Cruelty to Animals

A person who is abusive is often cruel to animals, especially if its yours. He or she is so insecure that any affection or love that you show to any person or animal makes them feel abandoned and jealous. The other motivation is that abusers thrive on power and control. Animals often cannot fight back. This makes the abuser feel more powerful. There is a strong correlation between cruelty to animals and domestic violence which is still being researched.

Abuse to Children

The abuser may be angry, stern and harsh to children. He or she may have expectations of children that far exceeds their age and maturity levels. Punishments may be excessive and unfair. The same controlling behavior displayed toward the mate may be also perpetrated on the kids. The mental, physical and emotional abuse to children may affect them for a lifetime.

'Playful' Use of Force in Sex

The abuser will often see you as a sex object, and that you should be there for his pleasure. Sex is not an act of love, but is a selfish act and display of power. He/she may pressure you to agree to forceful or violent acts during sex,

or want to act out rape or other fantasies where you are helpless. In many cases an abusive man will feel justified in raping you, he views you as his property.

Rigid Roles

Male abusers often have rigid gender roles. They may believe that a woman is to be subservient to a man. They may wrongly interpret the Bible, and demand absolute obedience, even in immoral or criminal matters. and should be aman may expect a woman to serve him, stay at home, obey him in all things - even things that are criminal in nature. Female abusers may verbally castrate a man who does not do what she wants. She may tell him that he's not a real man, call him a momma's boy or say things that are demeaning.

Verbally Abusive

Name calling, belittling, yelling, and cursing are common among abusers. The abuser often make cruel, hurtful remarks, both privately and publicly. The intent is demean and undermine the self-esteem of the victim.

Dr. Jekyll and Mr. Hyde

The Jekyll and Hyde personality is one of the reasons that individuals may stay in an abusive relationship. Abusers may have great public personalities, may be the woman's "dream come true" part of the time. The woman may rationalize that the cruel, abusive, angry personality is not the real person, and that if she conforms, he might change. There is a deep denial, as the patterns and cycles of abuse continue. How can a man who is kind, loving, considerate and generous also be cruel, harsh, angry rage-filled, even murderous?

Other Common Behaviors include:

Drinking and/ or Substance Abuse

Substance abuse does not cause violence, but it does increase the likelihood of violence.

History of Battering

A history of violence, or past violence is one of the strongest indicators that abuse will occur. Try to get information from previous partners, family members or police records.

Negative Attitude Towards Women

Threatening Violence or Harm

Breaking Things or Punching Walls

Force During an Argument

This is a huge warning sign . A push or shove can very quickly turn into a trip to the emergency room, or worse yet, he hurts you and won't allow you to go for treatment.

Review more online @
http://www.hiddenhurt.co.uk/warning_signs.html/ **public domain**

Why Are the Abusers Not Always Easy To Detect?

Abusers have what is referred to as a Dr. Jekyll and Mr. Hyde personality. The abuser may be an upstanding citizen. He may be the most courteous, attentive, doting person that you have ever encountered. He may be a respected professional in the community, or not. You may be flattered by the gifts, the attention, and how willing he or she is to spend so much time with you. Remember our story of Rachael and Gregg. He was the most loving, attentive person she had ever encountered. As a teenager, she did not recognize that his smother-love was control. He dominated and controlled her time. Whatever she wanted, he provided. She did not realize that he was isolating her from everyone else. His true colors came out in less than a month after they were married.

Once the abuser impresses you, hooks you mentally, emotionally sexually and sometimes financially, you might make excuses for the ugly behavior that begins to surface. Abusers always undermines the victim, making them think that they did something wrong. Victims will often walk around on egg shells, trying not to make the abuser angry. The abuser is already angry. I referenced the true story of a man who shot his girlfriend 14 times because she did not come home from work at the time he thought she should. As police handcuffed him and carried him away, he yelled at his dead girlfriend, "Now look what you made me do."

Why Don't the Victims Just Leave?

There are a myriad of reasons that victims don't just leave. Abusers isolate their victims, so there may not be any sympathetic supporters to help. The victims may be in love. They hold on to hope that the charming person that wooed them is still there, they just need to try harder. The abuser usually expresses remorse, often with tears and begging, stating how much they love and need the abused partner. They vow to change. There is a complex psychological condition known as Stockholm Syndrome in which women sympathize with their abuser in order to survive. It is sometimes referred to as Survival <u>Identification</u> Syndrome or traumatic bonding.

Sometimes cultural expectations such as those imposed by tradition and religion encourage women to stay and submit. I know of a situation in which a pastor told an abused woman to go back and submit. Her husband stabbed her to death in front of her children. Thankfully, now many pastors have become more educated on the horrible realities of domestic violence and offer better advice. Some women stay because they have no other financial resources, and they need to provide for their children. Also, some women stay out of stark terror and fear. The abuser is so controlling that he will often threaten to kill the children or family members or the woman herself if she tries to leave. Research indicates that women are more likely to be more seriously hurt or killed when they attempt to leave the abuser. According to the director of a women's shelter, a woman will leave the abuser and return an average of 7 times before she is convinced that she must save herself and her children.

Physical, mental, and sexual and reproductive health effects have been linked with intimate partner violence including adolescent pregnancy, unintended pregnancy in general, miscarriage, stillbirth, intrauterine hemorrhage, nutritional deficiency, abdominal pain and other gastrointestinal problems, neurological disorders, chronic pain, disability, anxiety and post-traumatic stress disorder (PTSD), as well as non-communicable diseases such as hypertension, cancer and cardiovascular diseases. Victims of domestic violence are also at higher risk for developing addictions to alcohol and drugs, depression…and DEATH.

According to the Center for Disease Control and Prevention (CDC), domestic violence is now referred to as Intimate Partner Violence (IPV). It is a serious, preventable public health problem that affects millions of Americans. The term "intimate partner violence" describes physical violence, sexual violence, stalking and psychological aggression (including coercive acts) by a current or former intimate partner.

An intimate partner is a person with whom one has a close personal relationship that can be characterized by the following:

- Emotional connectedness
- Regular contact
- Ongoing physical contact and/or sexual behavior
- Identity as a couple
- Familiarity and knowledge about each other's lives

The relationship need not involve all of these dimensions. Examples of intimate partners include current or former spouses, boyfriends or girlfriends, dating partners, or sexual partners. IPV can occur between heterosexual or same-sex couples and does not require sexual intimacy.

IPV can vary in frequency and severity. It occurs on a continuum, ranging from one episode that might or might not have a lasting impact to chronic and severe episodes over a period of years.

There are four main types of IPV.[1]

- **Physical violence** is the intentional use of physical force with the potential for causing death, disability, injury, or harm. Physical violence includes, but is not limited to, scratching; pushing; shoving; throwing; grabbing; biting; choking; shaking; aggressive hair pulling; slapping; punching; hitting; burning; use of a weapon; and use of restraints or one's body, size, or strength against another person. Physical violence also includes coercing other people to commit any of the above acts.

- **Sexual violence** is divided into five categories. Any of these acts constitute sexual violence, whether attempted or completed. Additionally all of these acts occur without the victim's freely given consent, including cases in which the victim is unable to consent due to being too intoxicated (e.g., incapacitation, lack of consciousness, or lack of awareness) through their voluntary or involuntary use of alcohol or drugs.
  - **Rape or penetration of victim** – This includes completed or attempted, forced or alcohol/drug-facilitated unwanted vaginal, oral, or anal insertion. Forced penetration occurs through the perpetrator's use of physical force against the victim or threats to physically harm the victim.
  - **Victim was made to penetrate someone else** – This includes completed or attempted, forced or alcohol/drug-facilitated incidents when the victim was made to sexually penetrate a perpetrator or someone else without the victim's consent.

- o **Non-physically pressured unwanted penetration** – This includes incidents in which the victim was pressured verbally or through intimidation or misuse of authority to consent or acquiesce to being penetrated.
- o **Unwanted sexual contact** – This includes intentional touching of the victim or making the victim touch the perpetrator, either directly or through the clothing, on the genitalia, anus, groin, breast, inner thigh, or buttocks without the victim's consent
- o **Non-contact unwanted sexual experiences** – This includes unwanted sexual events that are not of a physical nature that occur without the victim's consent. Examples include unwanted exposure to sexual situations (e.g., pornography); verbal or behavioral sexual harassment; threats of sexual violence to accomplish some other end; and/or unwanted filming, taking or disseminating photographs of a sexual nature of another person.
- **Stalking** is a pattern of repeated, unwanted, attention and contact that causes fear or concern for one's own safety or the safety of someone else (e.g., family member or friend). Some examples include repeated, unwanted phone calls, emails, or texts; leaving cards, letters, flowers, or other items when the victim does not want them; watching or following from a dis-

tance; spying; approaching or showing up in places when the victim does not want to see them; sneaking into the victim's home or car; damaging the victim's personal property; harming or threatening the victim's pet; and making threats to physically harm the victim.

- **Psychological Aggression** is the use of verbal and non-verbal communication with the intent to harm another person mentally or emotionally, and/or to exert control over another person. Psychological aggression can include expressive aggression (e.g., name-calling, humiliating); coercive control (e.g., limiting access to transportation, money, friends, and family; excessive monitoring of whereabouts); threats of physical or sexual violence; control of reproductive or sexual health (e.g., refusal to use birth control; coerced pregnancy termination); exploitation of victim's vulnerability (e.g., immigration status, disability); exploitation of perpetrator's vulnerability; and presenting false information to the victim with the intent of making them doubt their own memory or perception (e.g., mind games).

Domestic violence or intimate partner violence (IPV) is a crime. It is not a display of love. If you or anyone you know is experiencing abuse, DO NOT KEEP SILENT!

Need help? In the U.S., call 1-800-799-SAFE (7233) for the National Domestic Violence Hotline or visit the National Sexual Assault Online Hotline operated by RAINN. For more resources, visit the National Sexual Violence Resource Center's website:www.NRCDV.org

"No one deserves what happened to my sister."

Tamron Hall, Journalist, TV Host

"Live as if you were living a second time, and as though you had acted wrongly the first time"

Viktor E. Frankl

*"Get **your** soul fixed before you look for a soul mate"*

Toure' Roberts, Pastor and Son-in law of Bishop T.D. Jakes

CHAPTER 5

Are You Relationship Ready? Take My 7 Secrets Assessment

If we want to have healthier, happier, lasting relationships, we have to BE healthier and happier individuals. In order to better assess a potential relationship, or the relationship that you are in currently, my 7 Secrets story will help you to first assess yourself.

There are 7 basic, symbiotic categories into which ALL human problems fall. I have tested this concept many times over the years, with hundreds of people, and its truth is consistently confirmed.

Our lives can be compared to a garden, the 7 categories, like 7 plants. It is our individual responsibility to repair, nurture and maintain them. In the following story, an old man named Gardner reveals these 7 secrets to a young man named Kieron; and now these secrets will also be forever yours!

It was April in Alabama. The smells of blooming Dogwoods and wild Honeysuckles mixed with faint whiffs of Evergreens to form a fragrant, sensory bouquet as Kieron drove, windows down, around the coarsely paved, country road to Eliska. Gardner was dead and Kieron was going straight to the little country church to attend his funeral.

This was a different world from the fast-paced, stress-filled life that he lived as a businessman in Newport Beach, California. The Golden State had beckoned him after he completed a three-year tour in the Navy, followed by a degree in business law. His education had paid off; he was rich! It was in law school that he had met his Sue, his soon to be ex-wife. She had been a student at a nearby university, but one day she was on "his turf", doing research at the law library. When their eyes met, he instantly knew that he never wanted to be farther away from her than the next room. They were married a year and a half later.

Where had the years gone? What cold storm could have drenched the warm fire of their fervent love? Maybe it wasn't a big storm, just too many little showers: the missed dinners, his trips out of town, they're not listening to each other. He spent too much time away from the family, building the business, things just got out of control. Their two young children, Breanna,6, and Brian, 7, were suffering because of the tension. Sue said that he was 'emotionally disconnected ' from her and the kids. What did that mean? Emotionally disconnected?

Kieron was aware that his health was suffering also. Lately he had been feeling like a child, wanting to get off of life's carousel, but he didn't know how to make it stop. He was only 35-years-old but his rapidly receding hairline and specks of grey hinted 50.

Back here in Alabama, life seemed to have slowed down. How could the same 24 hours seem like 48 in California and only 12 in Alabama?

Upon entering the door of the cool, white brick building, Kieron took a long, deep breath. It smelled like home. He recognized the voice of his cousin, Dutch; she was singing the opening song.

"A-mazing grace, how sweet the sound"

A crisply dressed usher escorted Kieron to a reserved seat.

"That saved a wretch, like me"

Kieron relaxed.

"I once was lost but now I'm found Was blind but now I see."

His mind drifted back on the rhythm of the song.

"Through many dan-gers toils and snares I have already come. Twas grace that brought me safe thus far..."

He was 13 years old when Gardner moved a few yards down the road. His father had died 4 months earlier. His mother had explained how the lively 69-year-old was a third or fourth great-grand uncle or some genealogical combination that he could not remember. He immediately became fond of the wise old man with squinted eyes and an unsmiling but pleasant face. He looked like family, but different somehow.

It was quite fascinating to see how Gardner could laugh while hardly moving his mouth. It was as if he wanted his laughter to water his own soul rather than to have it float away in the wind. Gardner was not very tall, maybe 5 feet 6 inches; that somehow made him seem more accessible.

Kieron tasted tears as he smiled, remembering the many times after school, when he walked down the graveled driveway and hopped onto Gardner's front porch. He would be greeted by the sound of tinkling ice cubes swimming in sync with bright yellow lemon slices in a large pitcher of iced tea. With calloused hands, Gardner would carefully fill two large glasses, one for Kieron and one for himself. After taking big swallows of the sweet, amber nectar, the two would always go out back to a little patch of land behind Gardner's house where year after year he grew the same seven plants.

Kieron sat on the second row from the front. In typical Southern style, the casket was opened at the end of the ceremony. Even in death, he could not accurately distinguish Gardner's ethnicity. He had coarse, thick grey hair that used to be jet black. Gardner said that was because he had Indian blood in him. He attributed his almond shaped eyes to his Asian ancestry, his quick wit, Irish. His strong masculine confidence came from his African blood, he laughed. Gardner said, "Son, out of one blood, the good Lord made all mankind." Gardner had lots of 'words of wisdom' like that.

"...and grace will lead me home"

Kieron decided to not go to the graveside committal service. He would rather remember Gardner's life. He was not ready to say good bye yet.

His car seemed to automatically turn in the direction of Gardner's house. His feet instinctively carried him to the backyard, the place of memories that would last beyond death.

Eyes surveying the little plot of land that Gardner cared for so diligently and referred to as his 'Life Garden,' Kieron stooped down. He picked up several fists full of dirt and let them slide slowly through his hand. He gazed intently at the trickles of sand and small rocks as if they held secrets that would connect him to Gardner. Why did Gardner grow only seven plants in his garden, and why those particular seven things?

Kieron stood up. He looked at the withering Rose bushes, once full of vibrant, brilliant roses. They once made a floriferous semicircular fence around the periphery of the garden. The Potato plants lay flattened by the spring rains and the Runner Peanut plants were reduced to dead stubby stems. He looked at the spot where the Spinach was usually planted-only decaying remains. Even the usually lively Fig tree seemed to be in repose.

Opposite the Fig tree was Gardner's prized Anjou Pear tree. In its own private corner, supported by a crude trellis were the remains of his Muscadine Grape vines. This was the whole of the old man's horticultural occupation. Why did he call this his "Life Garden"?

Whenever Kieron had shared a problem with the old man, he would always counsel him in the garden, like the time he forgot his girlfriend's sixteenth birthday. She cried and refused to speak to him for a week. Kieron felt awful. The old man just put a friendly arm across the young man's shoulders and said "It'll be alright, come on let's check on the Roses, I think I spotted a few aphids this morning." That day, Gardner seemed to be extra patient as he taught Kieron how to care for Roses. He explained how they need lots of warm sunshine and a generous supply of nurturing with nitrogen, potassium and phosphorus, along with careful watering. Do that, Gardner had said with a chuckle, and they'll give you back lots of love in the form of beauty and an unforgettable aroma. Funny how he was remembering it all now; he thought that he was hardly listening that day so long ago. By sunset when Kieron headed home that day long ago, his problem with his girlfriend was not solved, but he knew a lot about Roses and, he had to admit, he felt much better.

Come to think of it, Gardner always had a way of making him feel better, like during those difficult days when he was dealing with his father's death. That counseling session took place in the Potato patch. Ugh! They had dug up a few Potatoes and thrown them into a sack. Kieron reached underneath one plant and thrust his hand into the mushy, smelly shell of a rotten potato! Just thinking about it almost brought back that horrible smell. As they washed their hands, Gardner explained that the Potatoes on that plant had obviously been stricken with deadly blight. He had to remove the entire infected plant away from the healthy ones or it would ruin the entire crop. The day he got the lesson on how to grow and take care of Peanuts was during the week of his eighteenth birthday; he was trying to decide what to do with his life.

Kieron took a long last look at this special place before he got back into his car to drive to his aunt's house to join the rest of the family. Upon entering the house, his mother handed him a copy of Gardner's will. The old man had left everything to Kieron. Through tear-hazed eyes, he looked at the signature on the crinkled scroll. Below his signature was scrawled, "P.S., Don't try to re-grow my garden; bid it farewell. And if you want the best chance for happiness in this life, you must be sure to take care of your own garden; it is your life." It was signed, "*Ted Gardner*"

CHAPTER 6

Take Care of Your Own Garden

Gardner was actually his name? He thought that the old man was called Gardner because of his peculiar 'Life Garden' with its seven different plants.

Kieron looked out of the wide picture window of his aunt's house. What did Gardner mean, "Be sure to take care of your own garden"? He didn't have a garden.

Instinctively, Kieron knew that Gardner wanted him to see something or *know* something and the secret was in the old man's garden. He kissed his mom affectionately on the cheek, telling her he'd be right back.

Scroll in hand, Kieron ran the few blocks to Gardner's house and into the back yard. He looked anxiously around as if for a hidden treasure. He had the eerie feeling that someone was watching him. He did not know what he was looking for but he knew that he would recognize it when he found it.

The door key was in the same place; under a rusty, upside down coffee can near the back porch. Inside the house everything was neat and orderly just the way Gardner liked it. What he was looking for was not in the house; it was in the garden.

Twilight was descending. He was seized with anticipation as he headed for the old shed at the edge of the garden. He stepped inside and pulled on the light string. Dim light flooded the shed. Perhaps Gardner had left some kind of buried treasure somewhere in the garden; maybe he left clues in the shed. He looked around. There was nothing unusual, just a lot of rusty old cans and sacks, thing that only held meaning for Gardner... wait there was something scrawled on the wall in the same handwriting that was on the scroll that he still held in his hand. It was Gardner's.

Kieron pushed aside a couple of bins that Gardner used to collect mulch. He wiped the dust off of the wall. There in the old man's handwriting were the names of the seven plants that he grew in his garden. They were listed vertically, and beside each was another word or phrase in parenthesis. His list looked like this:

Spinach (spirit, soul, body)

Pears (proper relationship with self)

Peanuts (purpose on earth)

Grapes (good health, mind and body)

Figs (financial prosperity)

Roses (Relationships with people)

Potatoes (Pains of the Past)

Revelation hit his mind like a tsunami. It seemed to wash away a veil from Kieron's eyes. He could not believe that it took him 22 years to understand what Gardner began teaching him when he was just 13 years old. He had not been teaching the boy about gardening at all, but about LIFE! No wonder he explained the delicacy of Roses when he had trouble with his girlfriend. *"Relationships are like roses; they die in the cold."* The wise old man even knew that the bitterness and anger that Kieron felt because of his father's death were like those rotting potatoes, infecting his soul. *"Bitterness in the soul, like a rotten potato, will infect everything it touches."* That's also why they always tossed the baseball or did pushups facing the grape vines: Grapes….good health. Kieron raised his eyes toward the ceiling. "Thank you Gardner," he whispered. As he looked up, he noticed a red tin box, the size of a shoe box, on the shelf above the writing. Among other things, he noticed seven little booklets, each held together with twine. He thumbed through them and recognized the now familiar handwriting that was Gardner's. He untied one of them and read the first few lines…..Relationships are like Roses, they die in the cold …another read…Rotting Potatoes are like Past pains, the blight infects everything it touches.

Kieron stood in awed silence for a while. Now he understood. Gardner had left him a treasure that was priceless- wisdom! He *did* have a garden, his life; and he *had* left his Roses (His relationship with Sue and the children) out in the cold. He had never talked to anyone about it, but he also had rotting

Potatoes (unresolved anger at his father, not just for dying, but for mistreating his mother while he was alive).

He tucked the box under his arms, turned off the light, closed the door and began to walk slowly back toward his aunt Roxie's house. By now, twilight was giving way to darkness, but he could see clearly.

His partner and friend, Keith, could handle the business for a while. Kieron had a different kind of work to do.

As he walked, the heels of his shoes seemed to be drumming an old song that Gardner sang or hummed constantly.

> *"Now let us have a little talk with Jesus, let us tell him all about our trouble. He will hear our faintest, cry and he'll answer by and by.*
>
> *Just a little talk with Jesus makes it right, all right!"*

Thirty-five year old Kieron built what had the appearance of a successful life for himself, but he had neglected and left in disrepair other crucial areas of his life. His family was falling apart, his health was failing, he was frustrated and miserable most of the time. While at his home town in Eliska, Alabama, attending his childhood mentor's funeral, he discovered that the old man, Gardner, had used his real life garden to try and teach the younger man about real life problems.

Kieron discovered that the 7 Plants in the old man's garden represented the **7 foundational areas of human life**. Each needs to be properly understood and maintained. He realized that he had given a lot of attention to his Figs (finances); but had sorely neglected his Roses (relationships) as well as his Grapes (good health). He began his journey back home with clearer vision and new determination.

This story illustrates the fact that success in one area of our lives, while neglecting another, produces imbalance, and prohibits true happiness and fulfillment. A person may have good mental and physical health, for example, but that same person may be extremely frustrated because they have no real sense of their life purpose and destiny. Kieron's financial success did not compensate for the neglect of his health and his relationship with his wife and children.

Alvin and Anita were both lawyers. They were well educated, physically attractive, and they had money. Even so, their lives ended in disaster, when Anita, his adulterous girlfriend, killed his wife. They both had serious character *faults,* not just *flaws*. They were deficient in other areas of their lives and it brought destruction and tragedy. Like Kieron, each of us has a duty and a responsibility to maintain, repair and nurture our lives so that we can be the best us, make the best choices, and stop hurting each other!

"Surely He hath borne our griefs and carried our sorrows"

Isaiah 53:4

CHAPTER 6

Meaning of The 7 Secrets

Kieron and Gardner's story illustrates a truth that was revealed to me that will share with you. This knowledge will help you to forever manage the garden of your own life, should you choose to apply it.

During the past thirty-five years of personal growth and through counseling and helping to hundreds of other people, I discovered that all of life's problems fall into SEVEN general symbiotic categories.

We may have a hundred scenarios, or situations, but if we can categorize them into their seven basic core components and learn to manage them, we will have a happier, healthier, more fulfilled successful, dynamic life on earth. The 7 areas must be consistently maintained, nurtured and repaired as needed.

SECRET NUMBER ONE - We must understand that WE ARE SPIRIT, SOUL AND BODY.

SECRET NUMBER TWO - We must have A PROPER RELATIONSHIP WITH OUR SELVES.

SECRET NUMBER THREE - We must know OUR PURPOSE AND DESTINY.

SECRET NUMBER FOUR - We must maintain GOOD MENTAL AND PHYSICAL HEALTH.

SECRET NUMBER FIVE - We must have SUFFICIENT FINANCIAL PROSPERTY.

SECRET NUMBER SIX - We must have harmonious RELATIONSHIPS WITH SIGNIFICANT OTHERS.

SECRET NUMBER SEVEN - We must be HEALED OF PAINS FROM THE PAST.

These Seven symbiotic areas affect all human beings. It is within these seven areas that hurts, abuses, disappointments and the like occur. Like a prized garden, our lives are in consistent need of Maintenance, Nurturing or Repair in one or several of these areas. Our neglect of these is wreaking havoc in the human race. We see its devastation in an avalanche of broken homes, domestic violence, depression, fear, confusion, pornography, drug and alcohol addiction, violence, anger, molestations, low self-esteem, sexual, verbal, mental and emotional abuse rejection, abandonment - the list goes on. Neither ritual nor religion have been able to impede it.

SECRET NUMBER ONE- SPIRIT SOUL AND BODY

Let's look at the first category and see what kind of problems fall into that category. As human beings we are spirit, soul and body. Hundreds of us neglect one or the other of these areas all of the time. There are those of us who are very physically fit, but our spirit and soul may be suffering, which will cause suffering in all of the other areas of our lives. Remember the seven areas of our live are symbiotic – different, but interdependent. This is also true of our tri-partite, 3-part nature. Our spirit, soul and body are distinct in identity, but dependent in function. If you neglect one, the others suffer.

Look at it logically. All of us know that going to the gym or working out vigorously everyday does not increase one's intellect. In fact that is not the purpose of physical activity. Likewise reading books and studying without exercise will not make you physically fit. These are activities that enhance your intellect, not your body.

Also, neither physical fitness nor intellectual stimulation alone will feed your spirit; it needs spiritual food. Among these are: Prayer, Meditation in the Holy Scriptures, and consistent Worship. This is our individual responsibility.

Relationship Relevance: If you and your partner have vastly different spiritual practices and beliefs, it will affect how and where you worship, how you rear children, and how you view and interact in all areas of your life.

THE SOUL

As a person, we are comprised of Spirit, Soul and Body. Research distinguishes three parts of the soul also. They are: Mind, Will and Emotions. Our minds take in and process cognitive data. Our wills make decisions based on this data or information, and our emotions are the feelings we have in response to both of these.

For example. I see a snake, my mind says "Danger!", my will says, "Move away from danger" and my emotions feel fear. All of these are actions of the SOUL. These processes happen so fast that they seem like one action and reaction, but our brains are so wonderfully and fearfully made and our responses so well-synchronized that we do not take note of the minute details of each process.

The Soul has perhaps been the most neglected area of 21st-century people.

People have had MANY experiences that caused them great emotional pain, and the pain still remains.

We put band aids on our scraped knees. We have surgery and take pills for our physical infirmities. But other than detrimental behaviors, the majority of our society does little more than take a pill to escape their deep emotional pains and traumas

If you want to have a happy, fulfilled and well-balanced life and relationships, it is essentially, imperatively, absolutely necessary to identify the origin or the root of your emotional trauma and obtain healing at the places of pain.

You can learn to find healing. If you or someone you are helping are too ill, or are in crisis, or an experience is too painful to handle alone, or is life-threatening, do not hesitate to go to a reputable hospital, psychologist or psychiatrist.

Relationship Relevance: This is the area where anger, pain, fear, grief, feeling of abandonment, rejection, and a plethora of emotions are lodged. If they are not properly dealt with, they will destroy you and all of your relationships. Rarely can we do this alone. Seek help for your soul- hurts, losses, disappointments, and frustrations.

SECRET NUMBER TWO-PROPER RELATIONSHIP WITH SELF

I am taking time to review these seven areas of human problems and experiences because it will help you to identify your problems, and then you can begin the process of repairing, nurturing or maintaining them properly.

You will no longer try to fix a spiritual problem with a physical remedy, or an emotional problem with a physical remedy, etc.

Having a proper relationship with yourself will either positively or negatively affect every other area of your life. Poor self-esteem and poor self-image have caused people to die from anorexia and bulimia, to disfigure themselves through numerous plastic surgeries and more. Poor self- worth has caused sexual promiscuity, repeated involvement in abusive relationships, lack of job success and various forms of victimization.

No amount of money, physical attractiveness, or even good relationships with significant others will fix the problem. In fact, many people have destroyed good relationships because they were not okay. You and I need to know why we don't feel okay. That's what I needed and I found the answer. If you were molested, raped, abused, rejected or abandoned, and it warped your self-image, self- worth, and self-esteem. You can be healed.

Relationship Relevance: If you harbor self-rejection, low self-esteem, unforgiveness toward yourself, you cannot love yourself or anyone else properly. It's a good thing to do self-care, not just physically, but mentally, spiritually and emotionally as well.

SECRET NUMBER THREE- UNDERSTANDING PURPOSE & DESTINY

People who don't understand their purpose - the thing that they do that is so fulfilling to them, so suited for them, that doing it is like constantly renewing oneself. Researchers say that most people have heart failure on Monday mornings. Some believe that it's because so many actually hate their jobs. We are programmed to learn a profession that will bring us good money, even if we hate what we do.

It is well worth it to take some time out, think about what you have a real passion for and find a way to do it either as a vocation or an avocation. Some professionals, even lawyers have changed their professions in order to find a more fulfilling career.

Relationship Relevance: Doing what you were created and put on the planet to do that makes you happy. If you feel happy, validated and fulfilled, it makes you attractive and fun to be around. Think about it. What do you really like to do? Is there any way to pursue it? Contact my office or another professional about taking an *'Interest Assessment"*

SECRET NUMBER FOUR-GOOD MENTAL AND PHYSICAL HEALTH

One Christian lady quoted a scripture, concerning her weight as she sat on the couch eating potato chips. "I will lose weight because the Bible says that I can do all things through Christ who gives me strength." The answer came back. "Let's begin by me giving you strength to throw away that bag of chips."

Quoting scriptures without applying action will not produce results. "Faith without works is dead." Some people over-spiritualize and neglect their personal responsibility to employ healthy eating, exercises and other common-sense health practices, such as drinking enough water and getting enough sleep.

We seem to be living in an age of 'magical thinking.' We want instantaneous results. Prayer does not take away our personal responsibility to do our part.

Magazines and the internet are rich with information on how to maintain good physical health.

We have to do certain things to protect our minds, so that the injustices, traumas and stresses do not cause mental illness that will incapacitate and further victimize us. Learning to process the pain through prayer, affirmations and good professional counseling will help to protect your mental health.

Relationship Relevance: In traditional wedding vows, there is a question, "Do you take this person to be your husband or wife, for better or for worse, in sickness and in health?" I have a friend who said that during that segment of his vows, he answered "for better, and in health." Most of us hope "for better" when we marry. It's unfair to burden yourself or a mate with a mental or physical illness that you can prevent. The unexpected can always happen, but we have control over many things that affect us and our relationships.

SECRET NUMBER FIVE- FINANCIAL PROSPERITY

You may be surprised to discover that a healthy spiritual life can lead to honest, legitimate financial prosperity. The Bible says in Deuteronomy 8:18, "But thou shall remember the LORD thy God, for it is He that giveth thee power to get wealth…"

Lack of financial prosperity causes stress and mental problems, and problems in society. But again, if we're not careful, we can blame other things and not get to the root cause of our money issues. What sense does it make to "get drunk" as a way of escaping your financial responsibility? Perhaps through feeding your spirit (prayer, reading the scriptures and meditation), you will get a God-inspired idea for a business, or an idea on how to go back to school, or get a trade. Read Joshua 1: 8. Remember, all seven areas of our 'life gardens' are interrelated.

Not only will attending to our spiritual health help us financially, when we are mentally and physically alert, we are more able to take advantage of any opportunity that might come along. Some people have sabotaged their own success because of poor self- worth or because they have problems with our next of the 7 areas, relationships with other people. Can you see how we need to diligently take inventory of all 7 areas of our lives consistently?

Relationship Relevance: I don't know about you, but no matter how high I feel spiritually, or how cute I look physically, or how in touch I am with my purpose, broke does not feel good. Lack of money can affect your self-worth and cause extra stress and duress on a marriage. Lack of adequate finances, have caused many unmarried women and men to compromise themselves, and enter into or stay in very unhealthy relationships. This is a trap. Financial independence helps you to not settle for a disaster-prone relationship out of desperation.

SECRET NUMBER SIX-RELATIONSHIPS WITH SIGNIFICANT OTHERS

This one is especially challenging, because most of the hurts that we experience come through significant others. It is also within the context of interpersonal relationships that we are forced to confront our own flaws. It is in this area where the Soul's battles rage. The will to forgive argues with the pain of our emotions. The memories of our minds fuel the feeling of our emotions, so that only the strength of our spirits are able to so influence our minds that our wills choose forgiveness over vengeance, love over hatred, and ultimately sanity over insanity.

The difficult decision to forgive is made in the courtrooms of our souls, but the crimes against us were most often perpetrated in the vulnerable arena of relationships with people we love. Holding them hostage in your own mind only hurts you. Anger and unforgiveness are causes of mental illness, drug and alcohol addictions, heart disease, cancer and other life-threatening maladies. A famous psychiatrist noted that if people could learn how to truly forgive, 85% of mental illness would be cured.

NOTE: Forgiveness is not as easy as just saying it. It is a cognitive process. It does not mean that the person who hurt you should not get retribution, nor does it necessarily mean reconciliation. Be sure to order my e-book, *How to Forgive When I Can't Forget*, at www.DRMINNIE.NET.

Relationship Relevance: I met a wonderful man once who wanted to date me. After we dated for about a year and he proposed, he disclosed that he had not spoken to his mother for 12 years. He further disclosed that he lived only 5 minutes away from her. This set off an alarm in me. I told him that I would definitely not marry him until that issue was resolved, and I wanted to know why it happened in the first place. My thought was, if he can ignore his mother for 12 years, how would he treat me after we were married?

Was this a *flaw* or a *fault*? It sure looked like a fault to me. Upon further investigation, including meeting her, I discovered that most of it was sincerely his mother's fault. She had abandoned him when he was younger, and every time he was in her presence, she was harsh and critical. They reconciled, and we got married. He was an amazing husband! We were married until his death parted us.

SECRET NUMBER SEVEN- PAINS OF THE PAST

Pains of the past are not in the past. Unless they're healed, they come with us into the present and will go with us into our futures.

Gardner compared pains from the past to rotting potatoes. Potatoes that have brownish or grayish patches and appear slightly sunken indicate infection with 'blight.' Such potatoes will either become dry and mummified, or rot completely. If left untreated, the disease will spread rapidly to other plants and, in a short while, all of the plants will rot and collapse.

An infected potato may look healthy enough to be stored with other potatoes until the unpleasant odor signals a problem, and is detected. The bacteria will cause decomposition in the affected potato and will aggressively destroy all of the other potatoes that it touches. This is clearly demonstrated in the horrible, raging epidemic of domestic violence. According to FBI statistics, more women are hurt and killed by an abusive partner or ex-partner than by drownings, car accidents, rape and murder by strangers, and victims in the Vietnam War combined. Read that again! This happens because the abuser has not taken responsibility to go through the necessary process to get his soul healed. Consequently, many young children see their mothers cursed, kicked, slapped, thrown down stairs, stabbed, shot and killed. It happens every 9 seconds. Physical, emotional and sexual abuse of both boys and girls are also common where spousal abuse is present.

'Blight of the soul' is caused by the unresolved, unhealed pain of traumatic emotional experiences. This malady robs the infected individual of love, peace and happiness and causes him or her to infect and afflict pain on those with whom they have close contact. I've heard stories that you would not believe!

I've looked into hundreds of tear-drenched adult faces who have lived for years with the pain of childhood verbal, mental, emotional and sexual abuse; men and women who were raped and molested by their own fathers. Women who have been brutally beaten, kicked, stalked, tied up and held hostage and more by their 'husbands!' The human soul was not designed to carry such a heavy burden; neither were human relationships.

These need to be fixed before we enter into a relationship!

Relationship Relevance: Similar to a rotten potato, many people appear to be normal, but repressed hurts, abuses and the like will eventually ooze out, contaminate their thoughts and feelings, and cause destructive behaviors. Without intervention, people who have repressed pain will decompose in various ways and will likely contaminate everyone with whom they come in contact. Unresolved hurts and pains of the past is probably the main cause of most *relationship destroyers*

"If you cry while you are healing, you are experiencing the cleansing purpose of tears"

Gerald Riggs, Paramount Pictures Executive

CHAPTER 8

Take My Relationship -Readiness Challenge

CHALLENGE & CALL TO ACTION

We are more prone to take care of the areas of life that are more obvious, such as physical health problems or financial matters, but matters of the spirit and soul are not readily visible, so those are often neglected except in extreme cases.

Transformation does not occur by knowledge alone, but rather when knowledge is applied. The following section is designed to help us realize that it is necessary to take proper care of all 7 areas of our lives, especially the PAINS OF THE PAST. These are areas of the SOUL (mind, will, emotions) that have been hurt, abused, abandoned, rejected and traumatized and which need to be healed if we are to lead healthy, happy, productive lives, fulfill our God-ordained purpose on earth, and have good, health relationships. Proper care of all seven of these areas of life will result in harmony in your Spirit, Soul, Body, and RELATIONSHIPS!

Now That You Know, What Are You Going To Do?

SECRET NUMBER ONE is <u>REALIZING THAT WE AS HUMAN BEINGS ARE COMPRISED OF SPIRIT, SOUL, AND BODY.</u>

CALL TO ACTION: Review the section on *SECRET NUMBER ONE*. Think about it and list 7 things that you WILL incorporate into your life during the next 7 DAYS that will help to either REPAIR, NURTURE OR MAINTAIN YOUR <u>SPIRITUAL LIFE</u>. EXAMPLES: 1. Attend an appropriate place of worship at least once a week. 2. Develop a consistent prayer life.

Complete the following 7 sentences as it pertains to your individual <u>Spiritual Growth.</u>

1. I WILL _____
_____
_____

2. I WILL _____
_____
_____

3. I WILL _____
_____

_____
_____

4. I WILL _____
_____
_____
_____

5. I WILL _____
_____
_____
_____

6. I WILL _____
_____
_____
_____

7. I WILL _____
_____
_____
_____

ACTION: Describe how you feel after writing these 7 things:

_____
_____
_____
_____
_____

ACTION: WRITE and SIGN the date that you will begin to INCORPORATE these 7 things. * Don't overwhelm yourself. Begin with one or two, feel free to apply these new actions in whatever way you choose, only do all of them at least ONCE within the next 7 days.

I (your name)_____will begin this action on:_____

CALL TO ACTION: Review the section on ***SECRET NUMBER TWO***. Think about it and list 7 things that you WILL *incorporate* into your life during the next 7 DAYS that will help to either, REPAIR, NURTURE OR MAINTAIN YOUR <u>RELATIONSHIP WITH YOURSELF</u>. EXAMPLES:

1. Recognize and Silence the inner voice that criticizes me by replacing it with positive affirmations. 2. Forgive myself.

Complete the following 7 sentences as it pertains to your <u>Relationship with Yourself.</u>

1. I WILL _____
_____
_____

2. I WILL _____
_____
_____

3. I WILL _____
_____
_____

4. I WILL _____
_____
_____

5. I WILL _____
_____
_____

6. I WILL _____
_____
_____

7. I WILL _____
_____
_____

ACTION: Describe how you feel after writing these 7 things:

_____
_____
_____
_____
_____

ACTION: WRITE and SIGN the date that you will begin to INCORPORATE these 7 things. * Don't overwhelm yourself. Begin with one or two, feel free to apply these new actions in whatever way you choose, only do all of them at least ONCE within the next 7 days.

I (your name)_____will begin this action on:_____

CALL TO ACTION: Review the section on **SECRET NUMBER THREE**. Think about it and list 7 things that you WILL *incorporate* into your life during the next 7 DAYS that will help to either REPAIR NURTURE OR MAINTAIN YOUR PURPOSE AND DESTINY. EXAMPLES: 1.Pray for clarity in this area. 2. Discuss this with someone who I trust. 3. Take an interest assessment.

Complete the following 7 sentences as it pertains to your Purpose and Destiny.

1. I WILL _____
_____
_____

2. I WILL _____
_____
_____

3. I WILL _____
_____
_____

4. I WILL _____
_____
_____

5. I WILL _____
_____
_____

6. I WILL _____
_____
_____

7. I WILL _____
_____
_____

ACTION: Describe how you feel after writing these 7 things:

_____
_____
_____
_____
_____

ACTION: WRITE and SIGN the date that you will begin to INCORPORATE these 7 things. * Don't overwhelm yourself. Begin with one or two, feel free to apply these new actions in whatever way you choose, only do all of them at least ONCE within the next 7 days.

I (your name)_____will begin this action on:_____

CALL TO ACTION: Review the section on **SECRET NUMBER FOUR**. Think about it and list 7 things that you WILL *incorporate* into your life during the next 7 DAYS that will help to either REPAIR, NURTURE OR MAINTAIN YOUR MIND AND BODY. EXAMPLES: 1.Begin an exercise program 2. Change my diet. 3. Find ways to relieve worry and stress.

Complete the following 7 sentences as it pertains to your Healthy Mind and Body.

1. I WILL _____
_____
_____

2. I WILL _____
_____
_____

3. I WILL _____
   _____
   _____

4. I WILL _____
   _____
   _____

5. I WILL _____
   _____
   _____

6. I WILL _____
   _____
   _____

7. I WILL _____
   _____
   _____

ACTION: Describe how you feel after writing these 7 things:

_____
_____
_____
_____
_____

ACTION: WRITE and SIGN the date that you will begin to INCORPORATE these 7 things. * Don't overwhelm yourself. Begin with one or two, feel free to apply these new actions in whatever way you choose, only do all of them at least ONCE within the next 7 days.

I (your name)_____will begin this action on:_____

CALL TO ACTION: Review the section on *SECRET NUMBER FIVE*. Think about it and list 7 things that you WILL *incorporate* into your life during the next 7 DAYS that will help to either REPAIR, NURTURE OR MAINTAIN YOUR FINANCIAL PROSPERITY. EXAMPLES: 1. Call and ask a creditor to lower my interest rate. 2. Pray for a divine idea for prosperity. 3.Give to someone who is less fortunate. 4. Seek a new job 5. Go back to school.

Complete the following 7 sentences as it pertains to your Financial Prosperity.

1. I WILL _____
_____
_____

2. I WILL _____
_____
_____

3. I WILL _____
_____
_____

4. I WILL _____
_____
_____

5. I WILL _____
_____
_____

6. I WILL _____
_____
_____

7. I WILL _____
_____
_____

ACTION: Describe how you feel after writing these 7 things:

_____
_____
_____
_____

ACTION: WRITE and SIGN the date that you will begin to INCORPORATE these 7 things. * Don't overwhelm yourself.

Begin with one or two, feel free to apply these new actions in whatever way you choose, only do all of them at least ONCE within the next 7 days.

I (your name)_____will begin this action on:_____

CALL TO ACTION: Review the section on **SECRET NUMBER SIX**. Think about it and list 7 things that you WILL *incorporate* into your life during the next 7 DAYS that will help to either REPAIR, NURTURE OR MAINTAIN YOUR RELATIONSHIP WITH A SIGNIFICANT OTHER. (This includes spouses, parents, grandparents, in-laws, children, friends, coworkers, etc.) EXAMPLES: 1. Sincerely ask for forgiveness for something that you said or did that hurt some else. 2. Do something for a significant other that you know they will enjoy. Order my e-book, *How to Forgive When I Can't Forget*, a great gift by the way!

Complete the following 7 sentences as it pertains to your Relationship with Significant others.

1. I WILL _____
_____
_____

2. I WILL _____
_____
_____

3. I WILL _____
   _____
   _____

4. I WILL _____
   _____
   _____

5. I WILL _____
   _____
   _____

6. I WILL _____
   _____
   _____

7. I WILL _____
   _____
   _____

ACTION: Describe how you feel after writing these 7 things:

_____
_____
_____
_____

ACTION: WRITE and SIGN the date that you will begin to INCORPORATE these 7 things. * Don't overwhelm yourself. Begin with one or two, feel free to apply these new actions in whatever way you choose, only do all of them at least ONCE within the next 7 days.

I (your name)_____will begin this action on:_____

CALL TO ACTION: Review the section on *SECRET NUMBER SEVEN*. Think about it and list 7 things that you WILL *incorporate* into your life during the next 7 DAYS that will help to either REPAIR, NURTURE or MAINTAIN YOUR AREA of HURTS FROM THE PAST. EXAMPLES: 1. Commit to *completing* this Program. 2. Find a good therapist, commit to at least 7 sessions.

Complete the following 7 sentences as it pertains to your Healing of Hurts from the Past.

1. I WILL _____
_____
_____

2. I WILL _____
_____
_____

3. I WILL _____
_____
_____

4. I WILL _____
_____
_____

5. I WILL _____
_____
_____

6. I WILL _____
_____
_____

7. I WILL _____
_____
_____

ACTION: Describe how you feel after writing these 7 things:

_____
_____
_____
_____
_____

ACTION: WRITE and SIGN the date that you will begin to INCORPORATE these 7 things. * Don't overwhelm yourself. Begin with one or two, feel free to apply these new actions in whatever way you choose, only do each of them at least ONCE within the next 7 days.

I (your name)_____will begin this action on:_____

NOTES

NOTES

CHAPTER 9

7 SECRETS Relationship Profiler

On a Scale of 1 to 10 -- with 10 being the highest -- rate yourself in all of the 7 areas below:

1. RELATIONSHIP WITH YOUR (Spirit, Soul and Body) _____

2. RELATIONSHIP WITH YOUR SELF (Self-Esteem, Self-Forgiveness, Healthy Self-View) _____

3. RELATIONSHIP WITH YOUR FUTURE (Sense of Purpose and Destiny) _____

4. RELATIONSHIP WITH YOUR MIND AND BODY (Good Mental and Physical health practices)_____

5. RELATIONSHIP WITH MONEY (Sufficient Finances, Spending Habits)_____

6. RELATIONSHIPS WITH SIGNIFICANT OTHERS (All)_____

7. RELATIONSHIP WITH YOUR PAST (Healing of Hurts from the Past)_____

If you scored lower than 4 in any area, I suggest that you make the necessary repairs in those areas before you deem yourself Relationship ready.

Rate A Mate

Take 5 deep breaths. Close your eyes and Make this declaration out loud BEFORE you respond to each item: *I seek the truth. I have wisdom and discernment. I reject deception, desperation and fear.*

Use your honest instincts, observations, intuition and discernment to rate a mate using the same formula.

On a Scale of 1 to 10 -- with 10 being the highest -- rate a mate in each of the 7 Areas

1. RELATIONSHIP WITH SELF (Spirit, Soul and Body) _____

2. RELATIONSHIP WITH HIS/HER SELF (Self-Esteem, Self-Forgiveness, Healthy Self-View) _____

3. RELATIONSHIP WITH HIS/HER FUTURE (Sense of Purpose and Destiny) _____

4. RELATIONSHIP WITH HIS/HER MIND AND BODY (Good mental and Physical health practices) _____

5. RELATIONSHIP WITH MONEY (Sufficient Finances, spending habits) _____

6. RELATIONSHIPS WITH SIGNIFICANT OTHERS (All) _____

7. RELATIONSHIP WITH HIS/HER PAST (Healing of hurts from the past) _____

COMPARE YOUR SCORES WITH YOUR MATE'S SCORES

WHAT IS YOUR RELATIONSHIP TEMPERATURE?

Is your relationship healthy and growing?------------
Call the Maid of Honor!

Or

Does your relationship need surgery?----------Call the Doctor!

Or

Is your relationship too sick to survive?-------Call the Coroner!

If neither of you is personally relationship ready, your relationship is probably

DISASTER-PRONE!!!

Take this opportunity to take my Relationship Readiness Challenge and make the necessary steps to being your best self, so that you can be your best in relationships.

CHAPTER 10

Components of a Good Relationship

What makes a good relationship is two committed, healthy people. I have counseled so many heartbroken individuals who cried, "I told him or her how my former partner cheated, or was abusive; now this one is doing the same thing!" Often people think that if they disclose to a new mate what their past mates did that was intolerable, it won't happen again. Just telling a broken person about your flaw or the fault in a past relationship will not fix the problem. The only thing that will fix the problem is fixing the problem!

With 50% of marriages ending in divorce, many people are opting to just live together. This does not solve the problem. When individuals join their lives, certain dynamics come into play. Research indicates that humans have an innate need to do what is scientifically referred to "pair bonding." I did some research, with references, which I will share with you.

Two Influences on Motivations for Pair Bonding

According to Broderick and Blewitt (2015), pair bonding is an adult attachment similar to the infant/adult attachment, but they differ in expression or methodology. Both relationships meet the basic needs for security, physical contact and exploration. In early childhood, the child/caregiver attachment meets the need for proximity maintenance, separation distress and provision of a safe haven. In adult relationships, the attachment meets the need for felt security, sexual mating and exploration. The primary difference is that the childhood/caregiver attachment is a unilateral relationship; the caregiver is meeting the needs of the child. In adult pair bonding, the relationship is bilateral; there is mutual care-giving (Broderick and Blewitt, 2015). Two specific motivations for pair bonding are for intimacy and to have a sense of security or belonging.

Two Benefits and Two Challenges in Maintaining Stable, Long-Term Relationships in Adulthood

Broderick and Blewitt (2015) cite various studies indicating that married people are happier, healthier, have higher sexual satisfaction and they live longer; generally, the financial benefits are also greater. Research indicates that the need of "we-ness", belonging to a secure union, is central and essential to feelings of security from birth to death (Broderick and Blewitt, 2015). This is one of the benefits of a secure marriage or romantic adult relationship.

Another benefit of maintaining a stable, long-term adult relationship is that it enhances exploration. Broderick and Blewitt (2015) note that this behavior is similar in both adults and children. Both feel freer to explore when they have a secure haven to which they can return. For adults, this may be of great benefit in career exploration or new business ventures. Broderick and Blewitt (2015) report that between the ages of 18 to 25, young adults seek significant romantic relationships.

According to both Holland's theory of personality development, and the idea of emerging adulthood, this is also the time that young adults are making career decisions (Broderick and Blewitt, 2015). Having the security of a partner might give individuals more freedom to explore options such as further education, job changes or launching a new business.

The fairy tale idea, "they got married and lived happily ever after," is just that, a fairy tale. Adults enter relationships with varying perspectives, cultural distinctions and experiences. Two challenges in maintaining relationships are the complexity of post-formal thought in young adults, and incompatibility in attachment types in adulthood.

Broderick and Blewitt (2015) report the work of Sinnot (1994-98) in describing the features of post-formal thinking. The essence of post-formal thinking is that it is relativistic -- adults derive at conclusions based on multiple perspectives. Some of these conclusions are contradictory. This kind of thinking and behavior can obviously cause conflict and confusion in interpersonal relationships. Broderick and Blewitt

(2015) refer to this phenomenon as it pertains to the helping profession as competing truth systems.

Hazen and Shaver (1987) developed a model that identifies adult attachment styles: They are avoidant, anxious-ambivalent, and secure (cited by Broderick and Blewitt, 2015). The **avoidant** type of individual is not very comfortable being close to others. They find it difficult to trust or allow themselves to be dependent on a partner. Their partners usually want more intimacy than the avoidant person is comfortable giving. The **anxious-ambivalent** types desire what might be perceived as an excessive amount of closeness. They often fear being abandoned by their partners. Individuals who are considered secure in their attachment style find it easy to get close to people. They are comfortable depending on others, and don't often worry about being abandoned. Obviously an avoidant person might find it annoying, difficult, perhaps impossible to have a successful, long-term relationship with a person who is the anxious- ambivalent type.

I have observed that many people go into relationships expecting their partner to complete or fix them. These unrealistic expectations can cause extreme distress and may lead to separation or divorce. Many other behaviors such as jealousy, being clingy and accusatory may accompany attachment types such as anxious-avoidant types. Avoidant types may not be able to provide enough intimacy to sustain a relationship.

How Environmental and/or Socio-Cultural Influence Impact Pair Bonding

Parenting styles affect the kind of bond that children develop with their caregivers. Broderick and Blewitt (2015) indicate that researchers have noted similarities between childhood/caregiver attachment styles and adult attachment styles. How children learn to relate to primary relationships and their environment carries over into how they relate to their adult relationships and environment. In some cultures, the extended is an integral part of a couple's relationship. Religious affiliation and sexual orientation can be big issues if one or both of the partners differ significantly from the community of the other. Broderick and Blewitt (2015) note that money and promotion are also external markers of success and will affect how couples live their lives.

Relationship Challenges May Motivate Individuals to Seek Assistance From a Counselor

Broderick and Blewitt (2015) agree with other researchers that all couples have conflict. Their findings assert that relationships fare better when the psychological atmosphere is positive. They generally deteriorate when the atmosphere is negative. Couple conflicts may include communication, finances, sex, infidelity, children, in-laws, work and many other issues. Some are more serious than others. Halrynjo (2009) cites research on the centrality of work in the life of men; consequently women felt "taken for granted." There were also problems with the men's role as father. When couples do not have the skills to cope with or work through a serious conflict, they might seek counseling.

Broderick and Blewitt (2015) outline the following core strategies for counselors who work with couples in conflict: 1. Calm down and be aware of your reactions. 2. Speak nondefensively and take a softer approach to the problem. 3. Validate, rather than criticize your partner; try to empathize. 4. Practice overlearning-learning responses that are self-soothing and that promote harmony. 5. Pay attention to the little things; notice and celebrate things that are important to your partner or that your partner does that is positive.

Rodriguez and Ritchie (2009) indicate that attachment is considered a working model, the attachment style developed in infancy will usually continue into adulthood, where the terms often become secure, dismissive, preoccupied, and unresolved (corresponding to secure, avoidant, anxious-ambivalent, and disorganized in infants, respectively). If two adults have extremely opposite attachment styles, they may need professional help in order to better understand and work with each other.

References

Broderick, P. C., & Blewitt, P. (2015). *The life span: Human development for helping professionals* (4th ed.). Upper Saddle River, NJ: Pearson Education.

Halrynjo, S. (2009). Men's work-life conflict: Career, care and self-realization: Patterns of privileges and dilemmas. *Gender, Work & Organization, 16*(1), 98–125.

Rodriguez, P. D., & Ritchie, K. L. (2009). Relationship between coping styles and adult attachment styles. *Journal of the Indiana Academy of the Social Sciences, 13*, 131–141.

CHAPTER 11

12 Relationship Killers: 18 Traits of Great Relationships

Attorneys and psychologist identified the list below as the top 12 relationship killers. The order may not be the same for every couple, but these are the common complaints.

"The saddest thing I hear in therapy is someone telling me that they've killed their relationship through what they have or haven't done. In fact, certain actions are relationship killers." Barton Goldsmith, Ph.D.

1. **Infidelity/Cheating**
2. **Money**
3. **Not Talking About Problems**
4. **Issues with children**
5. **Laziness**
6. **Opposite sex friends**
7. **Disrespect**
8. **Lying**
9. **Resentment**

10. Feeling unloved/lonely
11. Different goals
12. Selfishness/Refusal to change

18 TRAITS OF REALLY GREAT MARRIAGES:

Eighteen qualities that help make a marriage last:

1. **Trust**. Marriage space is sacred and private.
2. **Restraint**. Resist temptation and remain true to each other.
3. **Intimacy**. Be open with each other.
4. **Priorities**. Both put your marriage first.
5. **Difference**. Respect each other's differences, and know that difference lends interest.
6. **Sameness**. Share basic values, some interests, and tastes.
7. **Communication**. Communicate our needs, likes, dislikes, agreements, and disagreements.
8. **Fairness**. Play fair.
9. **Respect**. Demonstrate it.
10. **Emotion**. Be angry and sin not
11. **Reconnection**. Work out the differences, and re-connect.
12. **Humor** Laughter is good medicine.
13. **Gratitude**. We are so glad to be together, and we say so.
14. **Truthfulness**. Honesty communicated in love is honorable.
15. **Sensitivity**. Don't deliberately push each other's buttons.
16. **Persistence**. Be determined to stay married.

17. **Forgiveness**. Of yourself and each
18. **Teamwork**. Bring the best out

Published by goodtherapy.org, contributed by Dr. Lynn Somerstein

SURVIVING OR ESCAPING A BAD RELATIONSHIP

Remember Alice's story? She was at the hospital when her husband's mistress bore his child! She opted to stay in the marriage because she had been a stay-at-home mom to their 6 children. She knew that she could not care for them or provide for them by herself. She felt that her children needed their father's presence and influence.

Each person has to make that hard decision. One of my adult clients resented her mother because she stayed in a bad marriage for the sake of the children. That's a hard call. In the cases of physical, verbal or sexual abuse, that should never be tolerated.

When I asked Alice how she survived, her first response was a one word answer: PRAYER!

I can vividly remember having a traumatic time in the midst of a bad relationship. The mental anguish and emotional pain were so intense that I knew that in order to save my sanity, I had to immediately detach myself emotionally from him. It was as if I was in a parachute, heading for a certain crash. I cried, "Oh God, please detach my emotions from him and all of this pain!" I desperately pulled the rip cord in my mind.

That disconnected me from the downward crash and allowed me to float to a peaceful place mentally.

Some teachers refer to what has become popularly known as "**soul-ties**." Soul-ties are said to typically come from sexual intercourse. With that also comes an intertwining of emotions and strong feelings. The physical and emotional act of giving yourself to another person makes you very vulnerable.

In marriage, it is what makes the two to become one. In a healthy marriage a soul-tie forms an intimate bond that is nurturing and empowering. In a unhealthy relationship, it can be extremely destructive and complicated.

What Alice did was detach: she broke the soul-tie, and withdrew her feelings from her husband. They existed as roommates for the sake of the children. When her youngest child turned 18, Alice got a divorce. This was Alice's way of surviving. It might not work for many other people.

Take Care of Yourself

If you are in a bad relationship (not physically or emotionally abusive), you may have chosen to stay for your own reasons. My guess is that if you have been in this type of relationship for any significant length of time, you need to fortify yourself. Look at the **7 Secrets**, and repair, nurture or maintain yourself. Taking my relationship readiness challenge will strengthen you so that, from here forward, you can make your decisions from a healthier perspective.

I had a client once who was obviously beaten down in every way. I asked her why she didn't care about her hair and her appearance in general. She said that her husband treats her like a yard dog, so she feels like a yard dog. Although she was devastated and depressed, that spark of hope that is innate in every human being was still deep within her somewhere. I knew that this was true because there she was in my counseling office, seeking to reclaim her crown of dignity. I helped her to find it. Hallelujah!

If You Know You Have to Escape

If you are in an abusive relationship, and you have decided to leave, you have *to plan your escape* carefully. It is during this time that more women are seriously harmed or killed. The abuser is afraid of losing control of you. The ultimate control is for him to put you in a coffin permanently. You will need help from individuals whom your abuser does not know. This is definitely the time to call domestic violence hotlines such as the National Domestic Violence Hotline or local shelters or the police, someone will help you. This is not your fault.

You Have to Escape Mentally First

I recently interviewed the director of a women's shelter. She revealed that statistically, a woman will leave and go back to her abuser at least 7 times before she makes the final break. I mentioned Stockholm Syndrome as one of the reasons. Another factor is the soul-tie. That is a strong, illogical bond. You can't answer the friends and family who keep calling you crazy for not leaving that jerk. Both Alice and I prayed to detach mentally, emotionally and physically from the partners who were causing us such anguish. This will begin to break the soul-tie. It will be easier to follow through on your decision to leave for good.

"The best piece of advice someone has ever given me was 'do it scared.' And no matter if you're scared, just go ahead and do it anyway because you might as well do it scared, so it will get done and you will feel so much better if you step out of your comfort zone."

Sherri Sheppard
Actress, host of The Newlywed Game

CHAPTER 12

Beware of Depression

As I am finishing the final pages of this book, a young lady who is in her mid-30s, said 'Hurry up and finish your book, Dr. Minnie, I'm about to give up on love and dating and become a nun." Whether you are not dating at this time, ding on-line dating, or in a relationship, it can sometimes be very discouraging. Part of your self-care is to guard against depression. This is especially true around holidays.

Depression is a complex mixture of physical, emotional, and behavioral changes that can range from mild to severe, and are attributed to chemical, social, and psychological changes.

Depression is characterized by crying, anxiety, prolonged sadness, great despondency, inactivity and is often accompanied by thoughts of suicide. Depression affects 50-80% of the populationMany people experience an increase in feelings of sadness and depression during the holiday season. Commercialization of holidays such as Thanksgiving and Christmas often depict cozy settings of loving family and friends gathered in celebration. Valentine's Day is about love, which you may not be experiencing. This can be hard.

People who are not connected to family or friends, or who have had recent break-ups, or who lost loved ones during this time of the year, often have a very hard time during the holidays.

Another factor in holiday depression is SAD, Seasonal Affective Disorder. This condition is thought to occur when certain individuals do not get as much sunlight as usual, the weather is more gloomy, so people are less physically active, and they release fewer endorphins. This affects their mood.

People who have experienced significant loss or trauma around the holiday season -- with weather that can be cold and gloomy in our part of the world -- often say, "I HATE THE HOLIDAYS!"

Just as we are encouraged to prepare for the flu season by taking a flu shot, others take the old–fashioned, more natural route; which I prefer. They begin taking or they increase their intake of immune-building supplements such as cod-liver oil and vitamin C. So we have to take "medicine" to prepare for and avoid depression.

Resist Depression

This involves a conscious, deliberate plan that involves your thoughts feelings and actions. You do not have to just sit and wait for depression to overtake you like tidal waves from the ocean. You should become proactive and PLAN your attack against depression!A major factor in depression is the accumulation of negative, sad, or traumatic experiences which have never been properly treated. After so many sad life experiences and losses, or one or more major bad experiences, a person can become weighed down.

Medication may relieve some of the symptoms, but **it will not cure the root of the problem**, and most have very harmful side-effects. If you do not deal with the **cause** of your depression, it will not go away. If you are taking medication, I strongly urge you to accompany that with good counseling that incorporates forgiveness and healing therapy, and especially prayer therapy.

Here are some ways that you can **FORTIFY YOUR PSYCHOLOGICAL IMMUNE SYSTEM AGAINST DEPRESSION**

1. INVEST IN YOURSELF AND GET A 'PSYCHOLOGICAL MAKE-OVER'.

Find a good therapist, listen to some of the motivational messages of Myles Munroe, T.D. Jakes, Joel Osteen, Dr. Cindy Trimm, Joyce Myer and others; attend a good motivational or personal development seminar.

2. TREAT YOURSELF TO 'A DAY AWAY'. My prayer partner and I often go to a wonderful day spa, where we enjoy a sauna, steam room, facial masks, and relaxation and more…all for only $35 dollars for the day! Check around.

3. DO AT LEAST ONE GOOD DEED A DAY FOR SOME ONE ELSE.

This could include calling someone and asking them what their prayer needs are and actually praying with them, visiting someone who is ill, offering an hour or two of free babysitting for a single mom who trusts you. Men should do this also. It would bless the mother immensely. The list is endless.

4. **GET SOME EXERCISE.** Physical exercise, especially outdoor exercises, such as walking, jogging, biking, etc., actually releases your body's own endorphins, which make you feel good and boost the immune system. Maybe you can invite a friend to join you.

5. **RESEARCH "FEEL-GOOD FOODS"** Teas, vitamins and supplements provide the strength, energy and relaxation that your body needs

6. **GET OUT AND ENJOY THE FESTIVITIES-** Most churches have amazing Christmas plays, musicals, pageants, free dinners and the like. You might meet some wonderful people and develop some new significant friendships.

7. **GO HA, HA, HA!** Yes, LAUGHTER has been scientifically proven to actually cure diseases such as depression, even cancer. Did the Bible not say in Proverbs17:22 that "A merry heart doeth good like a medicine…"?

My friend -- the late Alice Arthur, Comedian and Joy-maker -- once said, "Laughter is the cheapest medicine that you can get over the counter - you don't have to wait for something funny to happen - **JUST LAUGH!**" Or even better, rent some belly-laughter provoking movies.

8. HAVE A PARTY BUT DON'T INVITE THESE FRIENDS:

Successful playwright, Edith Wilson, does a short play called "**MISERY HAS A PARTY**" ©. Miz decides to have a 'pity party.' Some of the friends she invites are, Dee, Zie, Loe and Sue. True to their names, Dee (short for Depression by the way) always sets the mood for the others. This inspires Zie, whose real name is Anxiety. Zie is always frantic, restless and on edge. It's a great party for Loe (Low Self-Esteem, that is). She is sure to bring everybody down, and Sue (Suicide herself) tries to convince the others to take the ultimate escape....you get the picture.

9. *CHOOSE* WHAT YOU WILL THINK ABOUT EVERYDAY

Bad feelings follow sad thoughts

When dealing with depression, sometimes it's hard to do "THOUGHT STOPPING," that is stopping the barrage of negative, fear-filled, dark thoughts about oneself, situations, events or anticipated events.

If not challenged, these **dark thoughts** will greet you before you get out of bed in the morning, and cloud, even control your entire day. These pervasive, ominous thoughts seek to hijack your mind, determine your mood and ultimately transform you into a shriving ball of helpless, useless, gloomy , unproductive blubber. Once captured by one or more of these tsunami-like waves of gloom, you feel paralyzed, overwhelmed, you are now behind this invisible, restrictive wall of darkness, as day after day you watch life pass you by.

"Don't live worried, frustrated or upset because of what somebody did or what didn't work out. Come back to a place of peace. It's not going to work against you; it's going to work for you."

Joel Osteen

CHAPTER 13

Ask Dr. Minnie

Am I A Sex Addict

Q. Dr. Minnie,

My wife of 3 years says that I'm a sex addict because I initiate sex with her about twice a month. We're in our late 30s; what up with that?

A. My guess is that your wife was raised in a strict home where sex was not discussed properly. Her parents may have presented sex as something dirty, and to be avoided for fear of pregnancy out of wedlock. In some cases women are not properly educated on sex. They grow up thinking that sex is shameful and dirty, even in marriage. F.Y.I. Normal sexual activity for a couple your age is at least 2 to 3 times per week. Tell your wife I said so.

Is Jesus My Husband?

Q. Hello Dr. Minnie,

My name is Lynn. I am in my mid- thirties. I really want to get married and have children. My friend, said that I should be content because I am a Christian, and Jesus is my husband. Dr. Minnie, am I missing something? Is Jesus my husband?

A. Hi Lynne,

Many well-meaning people have said that to other people. It sometimes causes confusion and some people feel guilty because they don't want to be unfaithful to Jesus. Let me just start out by saying *no, Jesus is not your husband in the natural sense.* If you are born again, Jesus is your Lord and Savior.

The Bible refers to the "Church," the collective Body of Christ, as the "Bride of Christ"; however this is not for an individual adaptation. God instituted marriage as an earthly covenant between man and woman. A distinction is made between that which is natural and that which is spiritual.

Do Men Have A Stronger Sex Drive Than Women?

Q. Why are we always told that men have a stronger sex drives and that women who fall to sexual sin were just emotional victims pounced on my bad men? Are all men just after sex and women just stupid or desperate?

A. Although this is a popular belief; valid scientific studies prove this idea to be ***untrue!*** According to the same studies, men are generally more straight forward about their sexual desires, women are traditionally more refined. This gives the impression that men have a stronger sex drive and that all men want is sex.

There are several other factors that help to perpetuate this myth. 1.) Men tend to be stimulated by visual images more so than women. Women are generally stimulated by words and characteristics that appeal to them emotionally. 2.) Our society is inundated with sexual images, especially of women. Television, billboards, magazines, pornography, the way women dress. In the American society, there are constantly images that are deliberately designed to trigger men's sexual urges. I assume that if you like vanilla ice cream cones with a drizzle of chocolate and a cherry on top, and you constantly see it displayed in various, seductive ways, you might talk about it more, want it more. 3.) Additionally it is an acceptable societal norm for men to 'sow their wild oats.' It is practically glorified!

These are among the many factors that make it very challenging for men who do not want to be controlled by lust.

Does the Good Outweigh the Bad?

Q. The man that I am dating has mostly good points, but he has one big problem: he gets angry very easily. Shouldn't I look at the fact that the good outweighs the bad?

A. If I were to make you a smoothie. I would start with orange juice, add a little coconut water, some strawberries, peaches and other delicious fruit, about 10 wonderful ingredients. If I pick up a dead roach from the corner who died from ingesting Raid, and add it to your smoothie, would you want to drink it? Why not, if the good outweighs the bad: 10 pieces of ripe sweet, juicy fruits, but only one dead roach. What's the problem?

You see, it's not the number of issues a person has, it's the kind of issues. Untreated, unbridled anger is a relationship killer, and sometimes even a potential person killer, regardless to the other "good traits"

How Soon Should I Have Sex?

Q. Dr. Minnie,

How soon should I have sex with a man?

A. As soon as you're married.

Cheaters

Q. My wife cheated on me after 8 years of marriage, I love her, should I take her back?

A. You should pray and seek a good counselor.

Q. Dr. Minnie,

I think my girlfriend is cheating on her man. He's my friend. I introduced him to her. Should I tell him?

A. I suggest you talk to her first. My first inclination is to say yes, but I don't know much about the relationship. How will your friend react? Someone could get hurt. I would talk to the girlfriend first, and perhaps encourage her to be honest and careful. People don't like to think they're being made a fool of.

Naïve

Q. Dr. Minnie,

My girlfriend is single, 25 years old, no kids. She's dating a guy, her first real boyfriend, who is at least 7 years older than her with 3 kids. I think that she should look for someone else. She is very naïve. What should I do?

A. Of course, it's her decision. Maybe you can just ask her one day, what are her goals and plans for her future. Perhaps you can then ask how this guy fits into that plan. It might make her start to think.

Commit or Not Commit

Q. Dr. Minnie,

How long should a person date someone before they consider making a serious commitment?

A. As long as it takes to make sure that they are both healthy enough for a winning relationship.

Liar

Q. Dr. Minnie,

I found out that my boyfriend lied to me. Should I break up with him?

A. You should definitely not ignore it I suggest that you discuss it with him. If he persists, you might do well to let him go. Lying and deception are relationship killers.

Here's What Oprah Winfrey Says About Relationships, from her book, *IN HER OWN WORDS*:

— "If a man wants you, nothing can keep him away. If he doesn't want you, nothing can make him stay. Stop making excuses for a man and his behavior. Allow your intuition (or spirit) to save you from heartache."

—"Stop trying to change yourself for a relationship that's not meant to be."

__"Slower is better. Never live your life for a man before you find what makes you truly happy."

__"If you feel like he is stringing you along, then he probably is. Don't stay because you think 'it will get better.' You'll be mad at yourself a year later for staying when things are not better."

– "Avoid men who've got a bunch of children by a bunch of different women. He didn't marry them when he got them pregnant, why would he treat you any differently?"

– "Maintain boundaries in how a guy treats you. If something bothers you, speak up."

– "You cannot change a man's behavior. Change comes from within."

– "He is a man; nothing more, nothing less."

– "Never let a man define who you are."

– "Never borrow someone else's man. If he cheated with you, he'll cheat on you."

– "A man will only treat you the way you allow him to treat you."

– "All men are NOT dogs."

– "You should not be the one doing all the bending; compromise is a two-way street."

– "If a relationship ends because the man was not treating you as you deserve then heck no, you can't 'be friends.' A friend wouldn't mistreat a friend. Don't settle."

– "The only person you can control in a relationship is you."

– "Always have your own set of friends separate from his."

– "Never let a man know everything. He will use it against you later."

– "Don't ever make him feel he is more important than you are, even if he has more education or a better job."

– "Do not make him into a quasi-god."

Amen Oprah!!!

Happily Married?

Q. Dr. Minnie,

Is anyone happily married?

A. Yes, but it's the ones who were mentally and emotionally healthy enough and committed enough to have survived the inevitable storms of life together.

There's Still Hope

*" IT IS MY CONVICTION THAT MARRIAGE
IS SUCH A GOOD IDEA, ONLY GOD
COULD HAVE THOUGHT OF IT."*

Myles Munroe

www.ingramcontent.com/pod-product-compliance
Lightning Source LLC
Chambersburg PA
CBHW072027110526
44592CB00012B/1420